erry
hristmas!
Merry
Christma

vol. 5

Park SoHee

About the Creator

SoHee Park

Birthday: March 24, 1978

She graduated with a major in manhwa from Gongjoo Cultural University. She won Seoul Media's silver medal for Best New Manhwa Creator in 2000.

Major works: <Real Purple>, <Goong — The Royal Palace>

Words from the Creator

A lot of people work hard to publish my book. Thank you. And a lot of people enjoy reading my book. Thank you.

Back when I was in school, I was really lazy, so I never finished studying all the chapters I needed to know for an exam. When I lived by myself for a while, I left my dirty laundry until it became moldy. I think the best happiness a human can feel comes when we are sleeping. I'm the laziest of the laziest. Thus, it's a miracle that I've been working on this comic's serialization so consistently and that volume 5 of *Goong* is now published. Thank you to everyone who has helped this miracle happen.

SoHee Park

*DAEBI IS THE WIDOW OF A DECEASED KING.

OF COURSE NOT. MY NOT LIKING DAEBI-MAMA HAS NOTHING TO DO WITH HOW I FEEL ABOUT YOU.
......

SO IT'S TRUE THAT YOU DON'T LIKE MY MOTHER...
YOU'RE TOO HONEST...
......

DID YOU HEAR? EUNUCH KONG'S GONE CRAZY...
WHAT THE—?! AM I JUST AN EXTRA?
HE'S BEEN STALKING PRINCE WILLIAM.

POOR WILLIAM... TSK-TSK-TSK.
YOU SHOULD BE HAPPY. NOW KONG WILL LEAVE YOU ALONE.

HA-HA-HA. OF COURSE. FREE AT LAST, FREE AT LAST!
STILL, SEEING EUNUCH KONG LIKE THAT...

AHHH~ PRINCE WILLIAM~
...MAKES ME...

...FEEL ABANDONED...
WHAAA?
GIMME A BREAK. YOU CAN'T PULL OFF A JOKE LIKE THAT WITH A STRAIGHT FACE~.
HA-HA. YOU DON'T THINK?
YOU LOOKED CUTE TRYING.

YOUR FACE LOOKS SO MUCH BETTER...
...WHEN YOU SMILE.
THAT'S THE REAL YOU, CHAE-KYUNG...

I KNOW YOU'RE HAVING A ROUGH TIME.

WHEN I SEE YOU STRUGGLING...
...IT FILLS ME WITH REGRET.

WHILE SHIN ISN'T HERE...
I SHOULD'VE ASKED MY MOTHER TO SEND YOU WITH PRINCE SHIN—
...YOU CAN RELY ON ME. IT'S THE LEAST I CAN DO.
SO PLEASE, DON'T AVOID ME—

YES, PRINCE SHIN IS IN THE MIDDLE OF HIS HORSEBACK-RIDING LESSON.
HE'S CURRENTLY ATTENDING A DINNER PARTY HOSTED BY THE BRITISH ROYAL FAMILY.
SORRY, HE'S NOT IN HIS ROOM...I WILL TELL HIM THAT YOU CALLED, YOUR HIGHNESS.

전체선택
선택해제
선택된 편지를
구분
첨부
NAME OF SENDER
Mail Deliver... Returned M
Mail Deliver... Returned M
いちごいちえ... Ichigoichie
Seung-Mok When you c
Song-Hee Jung Please join
Mail Deliver... Returned M
Pretty Boy Butter DNA It's Hye-Min
Peanut Sung-Ji Is William...
Da-Yun Pa Please intro
Soo-Bin Chae-Kyung
PRINCE SHIN FORGOT TO TAKE HIS CELL PHONE...
...BUT I CAN GIVE YOU THE SECRETARY'S CELL NUMBER.
OF COURSE I TOLD HIM THAT YOU CALLED, YOUR HIGHNESS.
PRINCE SHIN HAS BEEN BUSY. HE PROBABLY FORGOT...

WHY
AREN'T
YOU...?

OH, RIGHT—
HARRY ASKED ME TO GO TO HIS FRIEND'S BIRTHDAY PARTY...HIS FAMILY IS CLOSE TO THE ROYAL FAMILY, SO I HAVE TO GO.
THEN WE WILL PREPARE A PRESENT FROM YOUR HIGHNESS.

PRINCESS CHAE-KYUNG CALLED TWICE WHILE YOU WERE OUT...
......
THANK YOU.
MY PLEA-SURE.
CLICK
I KNOW.

I'M SCARED OF EVERYTHING THAT I DON'T WANT TO HAVE HAPPENED...

...THE THINGS...

I'M SUCH A COWARD...
WE'VE ALREADY SCOPED OUT THE PARTY, YOUR HIGHNESS.

OF COURSE, YOUR HIGHNESS.
NO ONE CAN KNOW THAT I AM BEHIND THIS.
HAVING CONNECTIONS FROM LIVING IN ENGLAND HELPS.
PEOPLE WILL ASSUME THAT ENGLISH REPUBLICANS ARE RESPONSIBLE. YOU SHOULDN'T WORRY.
NEVER—
HEH
SOON ENOUGH...
...THE CROWN PRINCE WILL FIND OUT WHAT REAL FUN IS.

WHY DO WE HAVE TO COME TO SCHOOL? IT'S WINTER BREAK!
I AM GLAD TO SEE YOU, THOUGH.

YOU LOOK ALL SAD, LIKE THE WORLD IS RESTING ON YOUR SHOULDERS...
HEY, WHAT'S THE MATTER? YOU LOOK LIKE...
...YOU'VE GOT SOME SERIOUS STUFF ON YOUR MIND.
...HUH...? DO I...?

NO WAY! ME? DEPRESSED?
씨익
SMIRK
YOU'RE FULL-ON BUMMED OUT!

UHH...THERE'S A RUMOR THAT THE NEW DAEBI-MAMA TREATS YOU BADLY. IS THAT WHY YOU'RE UPSET?

I DON'T KNOW WHAT HER PROBLEM IS...
...BUT I DON'T THINK IT'S HER FAULT I'VE BEEN SO DOWN LATELY.

THIS IS STUPID, BUT...
...I THINK... IT'S BECAUSE OF SHIN—
I KEEP CALLING HIM AND...
...SENDING HIM COUNTLESS E-MAILS...

I'M NOT SCARED OF...
...BEING BULLIED BY DAEBI-MAMA.
I'M SCARED OF SHIN'S COLDNESS.
PUSH
ALL RIGHT, WE'LL SEE WHO WINS THIS BATTLE.

I'LL SEND HIM E-MAILS UNTIL HE REPLIES, AND I'LL CALL HIM UNTIL HE ANSWERS.
I WON'T BACK DOWN UNTIL HE CAVES IN.
DID YOU SEE CHAE-KYUNG SHIN ARRIVE AT SCHOOL TODAY?
*500 WON IS ABOUT 50 CENTS.
SHE CAME IN A BIG, FANCY CAR SURROUNDED BY BODYGUARDS—WHAT A STUCK-UP SLUT.
I CAN'T BELIEVE A NOBODY LIKE CHAE-KYUNG IS THE CROWN PRINCESS.
SHE USED TO BORROW 500 WON* FROM ME ALL THE TIME~.

I'M SO GLAD I'M NOT IN THE SAME CLASS AS HER. SNOBS BUG ME.
THE OTHER GIRLS ARE ALL SMILES TO HER FACE BUT COMPLAIN ABOUT HER THE MOMENT HER BACK IS TURNED. THEY SAY SHE'S FULL OF HERSELF.
HER GRADES SUCK, HER FAMILY'S POOR— WHAT DOES THE CROWN PRINCE SEE IN HER?

I'M SO MAD THAT MY PARENTS' TAXES PAY FOR HER FANCY CLOTHES~.
SHH, I THINK SOMEONE'S LISTENING.

LET'S GET OUT OF HERE.
RIGHT, WE MIGHT BE LATE.

CREAK
끼익

꾹
PUSH
WSHHH
촤아아

THE ONLY PERSON...

...WHO CAN COMFORT ME AT A TIME LIKE THIS...

YES, I TOLD HIM THAT YOU CALLED.
DIDN'T THE PRINCE CALL YOU BACK?
I'M SURE HE JUST FORGOT. HE REALLY HAS BEEN BUSY.
HE ALWAYS FORGETS HIS CELL—
......
......
...YOUR HIGHNESS...?

CRACK
BASTARD.

DID YOU HEAR PRINCE SHIN WAS GOING TO ATTEND KADE'S BIRTHDAY PARTY?
YES, MY SECRETARY TOLD ME YESTERDAY.
HMM...I HEARD THAT SIR ROD BECAME PRINCE SHIN'S LOCAL SECRETARY.
WHY?
I DON'T KNOW ABOUT YOU, BUT THAT SEEMS STRANGE TO ME.
HIS FAMILY HAS PLAYED AN IMPORTANT ROLE IN THE ROYAL COURT...
I DON'T LIKE SIR ROD VERY MUCH. HE STRIKES ME AS BEING SNEAKY.

...AND AS HIS FAMILY'S ELDEST SON, HE'S AN IMPORTANT PERSON, BUT...
...HIS VOLUNTEERING TO BE PRINCE SHIN'S SECRETARY SEEMS OUT OF CHARACTER.
I HAVE A FEELING HE'S UP TO SOMETHING.
SIR ROD...
...IS MY MOTHER'S...
LET'S GO HAVE SOME FUN, PRINCE WILLIAM!
I SAID, LET'S GO HAVE SOME FUN TOGETHER~!
WHAT KIND OF FUN COULD I POSSIBLY HAVE WITH YOU?
HEE-HEE-HEE~! YOU'LL SEE~!

AHHHH, I'M GOING CRAZY! GRANDMA—
SEE YA...
ABANDONED YUL...
I WANT TO GO BACK HOME—
I TOLD YOU TO BE PATIENT. I AM BUSY. I WILL SPEAK WITH YOU LATER.
WHEN DID THE QUEEN BECOME HIDDINK*...?
*AN INFAMOUS SOCCER COACH
I HATE DOGS.
BRINGING THAT DOG IS ABSOLUTELY OUT OF THE QUESTION.

LADY KIM, TAKE THAT MONGREL OFF HER HANDS.
YES, YOUR HIGHNESS.

GOONG IS A SACRED PLACE, CROWN PRINCESS.
IT IS NOT YOUR PLAYGROUND.

WHAT DID I DO TO HER THAT WAS SO HORRIBLE?
IT'S IMPOSSIBLE TO GET ALONG WITH HER—
KNOCK KNOCK

AIEEE~! I'M SO HAPPY. I THOUGHT I'D HAVE TO LEAVE HER...
WILLIAM DISTRACTED MY MOTHER, AND I SNATCHED HER FROM LADY KIM.
HA-HA~. I DIDN'T REALLY DO ANYTHING.
BE CAREFUL NOT TO GET CAUGHT. PALACES IN OTHER CITIES ARE SMALL~.
LADIES AND MAIDS ARE ON YOUR SIDE, SO THEY'LL HELP YOU KEEP IT A SECRET.

THANK YOU, BOTH OF YOU—
YOU'RE MY EX-FIANCÉE. I'VE GOT YOUR BACK—
NO PROBLEM ...

WHAT?

YOU'RE REALLY SLOW.
I'VE GIVEN YOU SO MANY HINTS.

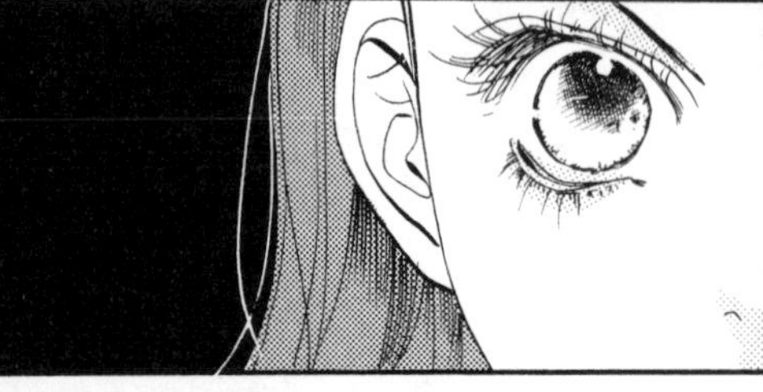

THE PERSON WHO WAS ORIGINALLY ENGAGED TO YOU...
...WAS ME, NOT SHIN—

PLEASE REMEMBER THAT...
...EVEN THOUGH I COULDN'T MARRY YOU—
EVERYTHING CHANGED AFTER MY FATHER PASSED AWAY.

...WHAT...?
BYE.

HERE I AM, BUT...

...WILL SHIN EVEN WANT TO SEE ME—?

THANK YOU FOR INVITING ME. I'M PLEASANTLY SURPRISED BY THE QUALITY OF THE YOUNG WOMEN ATTENDING. ONE PROBLEM: NO BOOZE?
IT'S AN HONOR TO MEET YOU. THANK YOU SO MUCH FOR COMING.
HAVE A GOOD TIME, MAN. THERE'RE A TON OF PRETTY GIRLS HERE.
HA-HA. DON'T WORRY. YOU CAN COUNT ON KADE TO SMUGGLE THE ALCOHOL IN LATER. RIGHT, KADE?

HMM...WESTERN GIRLS ARE REALLY GLAMOROUS.
THIS PARTY IS GOING TO BE, AS YOU SAY, "OFF THE HOOK."
THEY HAVE EVEN BETTER BODIES THAN ASIAN WOMEN IN THEIR TWENTIES.
HA-HA. YOU HAVE A BEAUTIFUL WIFE IN KOREA. YOU SHOULDN'T TALK LIKE THAT.

DON'T YOU MISS HER?
IT'S BEEN ALMOST TWO WEEKS.

WELL...

...SOME-
TIMES...
...I'M TEMPTED TO LEAVE ALL MY DUTIES BEHIND AND RUSH TO THE AIRPORT—

YOU'VE LOST WEIGHT AGAIN. YOU'RE MAKING ME ANXIOUS, YOUR HIGHNESS.
YOU NEED TO START TAKING A NEW HERBAL VITAMIN RIGHT AWAY.

I AM IN CHARGE OF YOUR HEALTH.
IF YOU KEEP LOSING WEIGHT, I WILL BE IN TROUBLE WITH THE CROWN PRINCE.

PLEASE DON'T WORRY. THE CROWN PRINCE DOESN'T CARE ABOUT MY HEALTH AT ALL.

OH!
WERE PRINCE YUL AND I...
YES? WHAT...?
I MEAN...

OH, IT'S NOTHING—
...SHE TOLD ME THAT A MILLION TIMES, BUT...
...HER WARNINGS WON'T STOP ME~.
YOU SHOULD NEVER GO TO BUILDINGS ON THE PERIMETER, YOUR HIGHNESS.
THE SECURITY OF THE OUTER BUILDINGS IS NOT AS TIGHT AS IT IS TOWARD THE CENTER.
WOW~ THE SKY'S REALLY CLEAR— THE WEATHER'S QUITE WARM FOR A WINTER DAY.
*THIS PALACE IS LOCATED IN KIMHAE. IT WAS BUILT AFTER THE LIBERATION FROM JAPAN.

I WONDER, IS WHAT YUL SAID TRUE?
WHAT'S THAT?
WE USED TO BE ENGAGED? YUL AND ME...?
WAHHH! I WANT MY BALLOON BACK! PLEASE, MOMMY~!
DON'T DO THAT! YOU'LL ATTRACT PALACE SECURITY!

JUST A LITTLE HIGHER~
AHH~

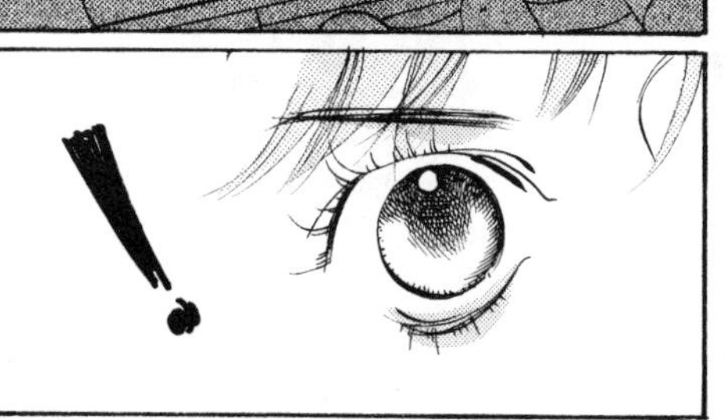
!

UH...
HURRY UP. WHAT'S TAKING SO LONG?
OKAY, OKAY, MOM~.

SHHH
쉬잇
으랏차
TUG
HERE.
HEY, HYE-MIN. MOMMY'S ARMS ARE DYING!
OKAY, MOM~.
THANK YOU, PRETTY PRINCESS~!

I WANT TO BE...
...ON THE OTHER SIDE OF THIS WALL—

ALL THE THINGS I USED TO DO OUTSIDE THESE WALLS...
...WALKING DOWN THE STREET ON A SUNNY DAY, RIDING A BUSY SUBWAY TRAIN, WATCHING A MOVIE AFTER WAITING IN A LONG LINE...

THOSE THINGS USED TO BE A PART OF MY LIFE.
BUT NOW...
...I MISS MY SIMPLE EXISTENCE...

I'M BUZZED—DID SOMEONE SPIKE THE PUNCH?
WHOA. IS THIS A NON-ALCOHOLIC DRINK? 'COS I FEEL WEIRD.
NO, THIS ISN'T AN ALCOHOL BUZZ. I DON'T KNOW HOW TO SAY IT...I FEEL LIKE I'M STONED...
WHATEVER. HAVE MORE. IT WON'T KILL US.
RIGHT, FILL 'ER UP FOR ME PLEASE. HA-HA-HA.

HEH-HEH-HEH... GLAD YOU'RE ENJOYING THE REFRESHMENTS, CROWN PRINCE.
MARTIN.
YES, SIR.
LET'S GET READY TO CALL THE POLICE.
YES, SIR.

COURT LADIES AND MAIDS BELONGED TO THE NAEMYUNG-BU (A GENERAL TERM FOR PALACE WOMEN IN THE CHOSUN DYNASTY), AND THEY WORKED IN DIFFERENT DEPARTMENTS, INCLUDING JIMIL (MAINTAINING THE KING AND QUEEN'S QUARTERS), CHIMBANG (MAKING CLOTHES), SOOBANG (EMBROIDERY), SESOOGAN (FETCHING WATER FOR BATHS AND WASHING), SOJUBANG (COOKING), AND SANGGWABANG (MAKING DESSERTS AND SNACKS).

THESE DAYS, COURT LADIES MUST PASS A TEST AND ARE TREATED LIKE OFFICERS IN THE PALACE, RECEIVING MONETARY COMPENSATION. IF THEY WANT TO GET MARRIED, HOWEVER, THEY HAVE TO GIVE UP THEIR POSITIONS AND LEAVE THE PALACE.

YAWN, I'M TIRED.
I WILL BRING YOUR HERBS. I WANT YOU TO TAKE THEM BEFORE YOU NAP.

AHH~! I DON'T LIKE HERBS~!
YOUR HIGHNESS.
OKAY, I'LL TAKE THEM IN A WHILE~.

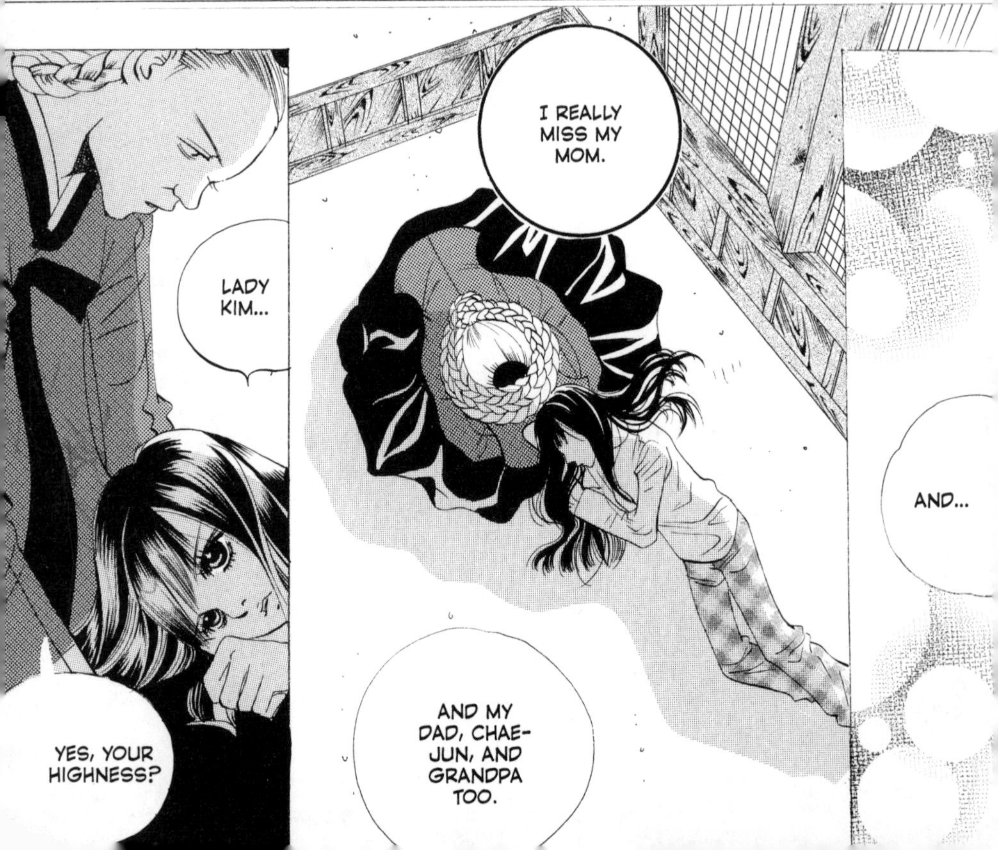
LADY KIM...
YES, YOUR HIGHNESS?
I REALLY MISS MY MOM.
AND MY DAD, CHAE-JUN, AND GRANDPA TOO.
AND...

...I REALLY MISS SHIN.

YOU HAVE TO BE STRONG, YOUR HIGHNESS.

POOR PRINCESS CHAE-KYUNG. SHE WAS MARRIED AT SUCH A YOUNG AGE.
SHE HAS NO ONE TO RELY ON IN THE PALACE. MOREOVER, THE NEW DAEBI IS SO UNKIND...

YOUR BODY IS NOT YOURS ALONE.

YOUR BODY IS PRECIOUS TO ALL THE PEOPLE, BECAUSE ONE DAY YOU WILL BECOME THE QUEEN OF THIS COUNTRY.
!

Q-QUEEN...?
TECH-NICALLY...

...THE CROWN PRINCESS IS ALWAYS IN THE PROCESS OF BECOMING THE NEXT QUEEN.
YOU MAY NOT BECOME QUEEN IN THE NEAR FUTURE, BUT IN A FEW YEARS...

...YOU WILL BE THE MOTHER OF A ROYAL GRANDSON WHO WILL BE KING AFTER PRINCE SHIN—
EH...? M-MOTHER... GRAND-SON?
KING AND QUEEN?
I'LL BE THE MOTHER OF A BABY—?!

WOMEN OF THE ROYAL FAMILY GENERALLY HAVE BABIES AT AN EARLY AGE—
THAT'S BECAUSE SOMETHING HAPPENS SOONER THAN IT DOES FOR OTHER PEOPLE. MWA-HA-HA-HA...
D-DON'T SAY STUFF LIKE THAT! AND STOP LAUGHING!
WHAT'S WITH THAT SNEAKY LAUGH?!
OF COURSE, YOUR HIGHNESS.
NOT JUST ANY BABY, THOUGH...
WHEN YOU AND PRINCE SHIN BECOME ADULTS, THE ROYAL FAMILY AND PEOPLE OF KOREA WILL BE WAITING FOR A ROYAL GRANDSON'S ARRIVAL.
*REAL NAME OF A POPULAR INSTANT RAMEN
OOO
GAHHH
허걱
HAPPY SHIN RAMEN* FAMILY
HA-HA-HA... THIS IS OUR LITTLE PUPPY~

HEH-HEH-HEH-HEH...
SOMETHING? SOMETHING?
I WONDER WHAT THAT SOMETHING IS...
HEH-HEH-HEH-HEH...

WAIT A MINUTE...

I REALLY LIKE SHIN, BUT I GUESS I HAVE TO DIVORCE HIM BEFORE WE BECOME ADULTS...
휘릭~
TURN

...YOU'RE ACCUSING ME OF BRINGING ILLEGAL DRUGS HERE?
S-SO...
ARE YOU OUT OF YOUR MIND—?

WE FOUND THESE IN YOUR BAG AND YOUR JACKET.
SOMEONE CALLED THE POLICE WITHOUT KNOWING THAT THEY WERE YOURS.

WE WANT TO BELIEVE THAT YOU AREN'T RESPONSIBLE FOR BRINGING THEM HERE.

BUT WE STILL HAVE TO ASK YOU SOME QUESTIONS. PLEASE COOPERATE WITH US.

WHERE'S SIR ROD? HE AND I CAME TOGETHER...
...AND HE NEEDS TO EXPLAIN THIS TO THEM.

WELL... WE HAVE BEEN LOOKING FOR HIM, BUT...
...IT SEEMS HE ALREADY LEFT. WE KEEP CALLING HIM, BUT...
HE VANISHED BEFORE THE POLICE ARRIVED...
IT'S NOT APPROPRIATE FOR A SECRETARY TO ABANDON HIS CHARGE AT A TIME LIKE THIS.
I'M HAVING TROUBLE TAKING THIS ALL IN. SIR ROD IS HANDLING ALL MY BELONGINGS...
...SO I WILL TALK TO YOU ONCE HE RETURNS.

SLAM
WHAT DO YOU MEAN—?!

THE ENGLISH POLICE ARE INVESTIGATING THE INCIDENT WITHOUT INFORMING THE MEDIA.
PRINCE SHIN WAS INTERROGATED AT BUCKINGHAM PALACE.

IS THERE ANY PROGRESS IN THE INVESTIGATION?

TH-THAT IS... NOT YET...
THERE WERE TOO MANY PEOPLE AT THE PARTY, AND NO ONE KNOWS EXACTLY WHAT HAPPENED.

PRINCE SHIN WOULD NEVER DO SUCH A THING.
SOMEONE MUST HAVE FRAMED HIM.
I KNOW. I AM SURE SHIN IS INNOCENT.
THERE IS NO WAY SHIN COULD HAVE BOUGHT SO MUCH MARIJUANA AND ILLEGAL NARCOTICS, BUT...
...WHY DID IT HAPPEN TO HIM—?
WHY DOES THIS KIND OF THING ALWAYS HAPPEN TO SHIN?
THE BRITISH HAVE KEPT THE PRESS IN THE DARK ABOUT THIS. EVEN IF THE STORY LEAKS, THE PAPERS WILL TREAD CAUTIOUSLY. IT'S TOO BIG.
BUT THAT IS NOT WHAT'S REALLY IMPORTANT HERE.

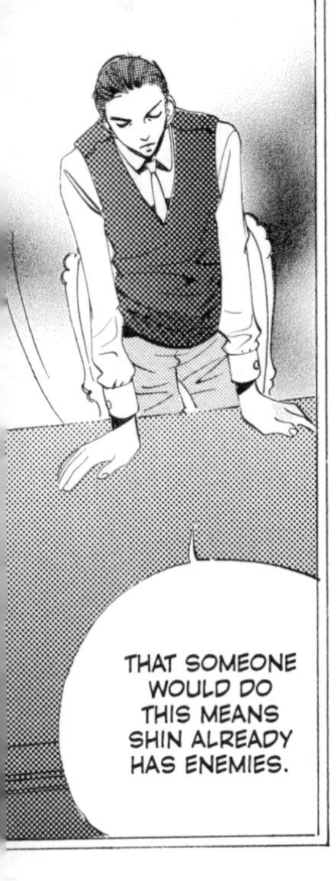
THAT SOMEONE WOULD DO THIS MEANS SHIN ALREADY HAS ENEMIES.

SHIN'S ENEMIES ARE VERY POWERFUL IF THEY CAN PULL OFF SUCH A DEVIOUS TRICK SO EASILY. I AM NOT SURE SHIN CAN RULE KOREA.
!

WHAT ARE YOU GOING TO DO...?

ARE YOU GOING TO RENAME THE CROWN PRINCE AND APPOINT YUL?

IT'S NOT IMPOSSIBLE—

THIS INCIDENT IS MY FAULT.
I AM SO SORRY, YOUR HIGHNESS.
I HAVE PUT YOU IN A DIFFICULT POSITION.

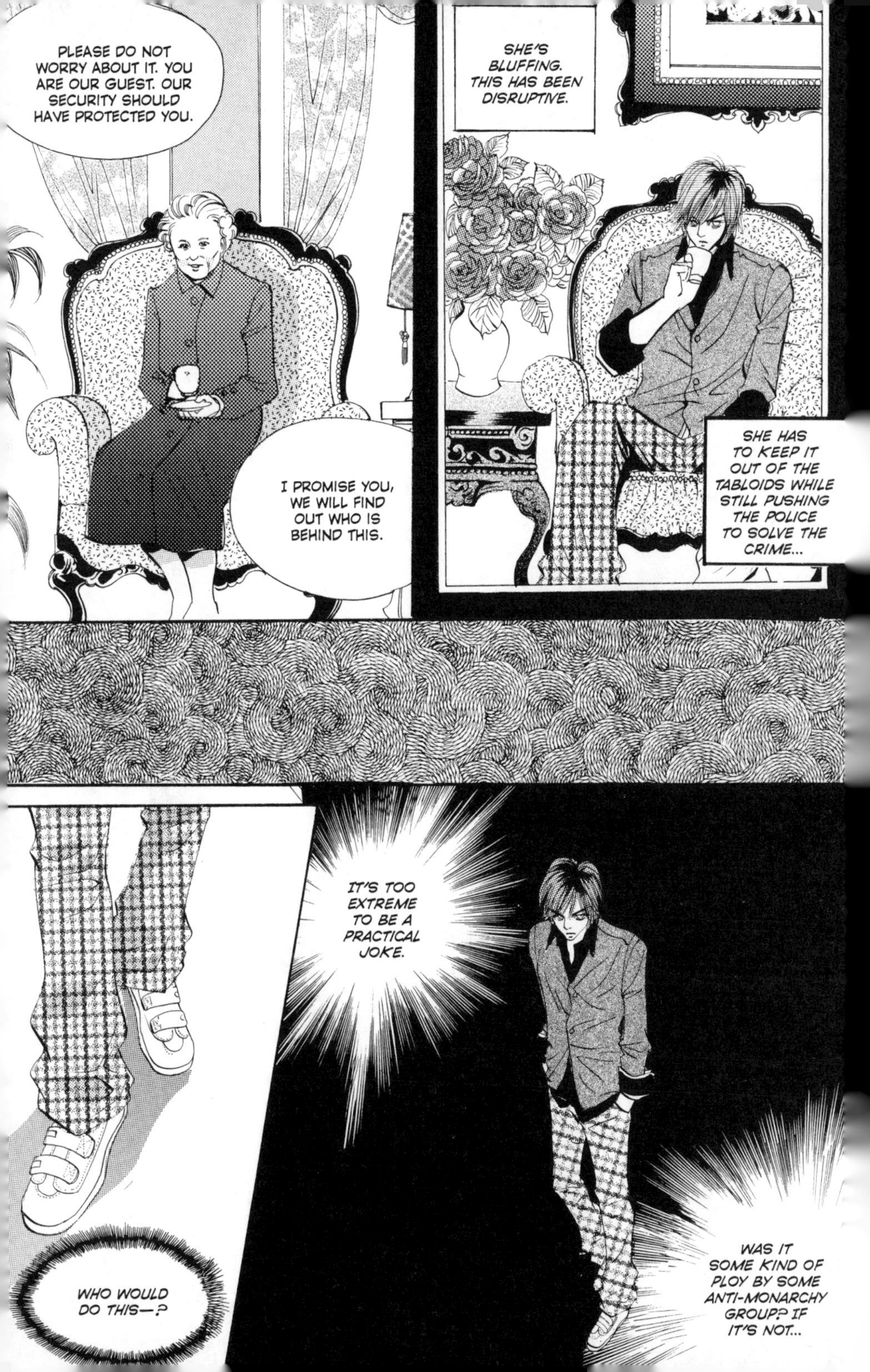
PLEASE DO NOT WORRY ABOUT IT. YOU ARE OUR GUEST. OUR SECURITY SHOULD HAVE PROTECTED YOU.
I PROMISE YOU, WE WILL FIND OUT WHO IS BEHIND THIS.
SHE'S BLUFFING. THIS HAS BEEN DISRUPTIVE.
SHE HAS TO KEEP IT OUT OF THE TABLOIDS WHILE STILL PUSHING THE POLICE TO SOLVE THE CRIME...
WHO WOULD DO THIS—?
IT'S TOO EXTREME TO BE A PRACTICAL JOKE.
WAS IT SOME KIND OF PLOY BY SOME ANTI-MONARCHY GROUP? IF IT'S NOT...

UH...YOUR HIGHNESS, I MUST SPEAK TO YOU ABOUT SIR ROD...
WHAT IS IT?

UHH... THERE'S SOMETHING STRANGE ABOUT HIM.
IT MAY HAVE NOTHING TO DO WITH THE SCANDAL, BUT...

...WHEN DAEBI-MAMA STAYED IN ENGLAND, SHE WAS VERY CLOSE TO HIM.
SO WHAT? SHE HAS MANY FRIENDS IN ENGLISH HIGH SOCIETY.

BUT NONE OF THOSE FRIENDS VOLUNTEERED TO BE YOUR LOCAL SECRETARY.

AND HE IS THE ONE WHO RECOMMENDED WE SEND LILIES TO QUEEN ELIZABETH.
IF HER MAIDS HADN'T CORRECTED US, IT WOULD'VE BEEN A HUGE DISASTER.

HE TOLD US LILIES WERE THE QUEEN'S FAVORITE, BUT THE MAIDS TOLD US THEY REPRESENT DEATH IN BRITISH CULTURE.
I HAVE A HARD TIME BELIEVING HE DIDN'T KNOW.

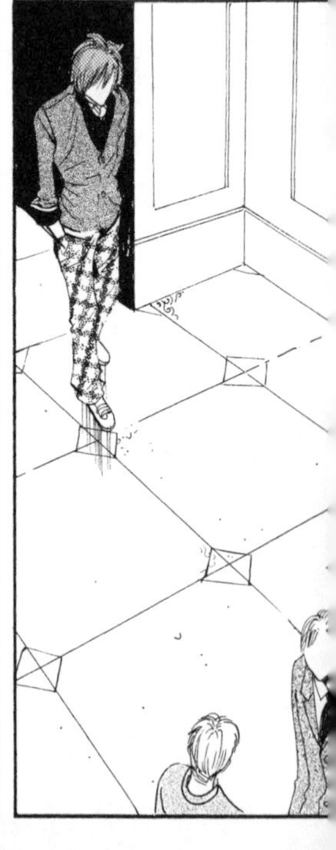

SIR ROD—
OH, YOUR HIGHNESS—
YOU'RE A HARD MAN TO GET A HOLD OF. HAVE YOU BEEN BUSY?
AH, YES...I'VE BEEN WORKING TO QUELL ANY RUMORS THAT SPREAD ABOUT THAT PARTY.
I JUST CAME BACK FROM NEW SCOTLAND YARD.

I MET UP WITH ADAM AND ASKED HIM TO HANDLE THIS INVESTIGATION WITH DISCREET EFFICIENCY.
YOU MEAN... CAPTAIN ADAM? SHORT, WITH A MUSTACHE, RIGHT?
YES, YOUR HIGHNESS. HE IS A RELIABLE MAN.
CAPTAIN ADAM IS WITH HER MAJESTY RIGHT NOW—
HMM... THAT'S STRANGE.

......
DOES HE—?
LATER, THEN—
DOES HE HAVE A TWIN?
HA.

THE VISITOR IS IN THE OUTER BUILDING. WOULD YOU LIKE TO GO SEE?
SOMEONE IS HERE TO SEE ME?
YES, YOUR HIGHNESS. I HAVE SEEN HER AT THE SCHOOL SEVERAL TIMES. I THOUGHT SHE WAS A FRIEND OF YOURS—
A FRIEND WHO CAME ALL THE WAY TO ENGLAND TO SEE ME...?

UHH...

I LIED AND TOLD MY MOM I WAS GOING TO PARIS TO SEE THE WORLD BALLET COMPETITION.
I HAD TO BREAK INTO THE SAVINGS ACCOUNT I'VE HAD SINCE GRADE SCHOOL.
HEH.
?
THIS IS SO LIKE YOU, HYO-RIN.
BY THE WAY, SHIN...
...WHAT'S UP WITH THIS SAD FACE? IS THERE A PROBLEM?
I'M FINE. THE FOOD HERE JUST DOESN'T AGREE WITH ME...

I HAVE NO MONEY TO GET BACK—
WHERE ARE YOU STAYING? ARE YOU IN PICCADILLY CIRCUS?
HOW SHOULD I PUT THIS...?
ARE YOU CRAZY—?
WHAT DID YOU JUST SAY—?!

YES.
I LOVE CHAE-KYUNG.
SHE IS MARRIED!
SHE IS YOUR COUSIN'S WIFE!
SHE USED TO BE MY FIANCÉE.
SHIN IS THE ONE WHO TOOK HER FROM ME.

I CAN'T BELIEVE THIS. WHEN YOUR FATHER PASSED AWAY...
...THE ONLY POSITIVE THING TO COME FROM IT WAS THAT YOU DIDN'T HAVE TO MARRY THAT STUPID GIRL!
BUT WHAT DID YOU JUST SAY?
YOU LOVE HER—?!
STRANGE THING IS...
...YOUR DISAPPROVAL MAKES ME LOVE HER MORE.
YOU THOUGHT I DIDN'T KNOW? ONE OF THE REASONS YOU LEFT CHAE-KYUNG BEHIND IN THE PALACE IN KIMHAE...
...WAS TO SEPARATE HER FROM ME.
O-OF COURSE NOT! SHE HAS LIVED IN SEOUL HER WHOLE LIFE, SO SHE HAS A LOT TO LEARN ABOUT THE DIFFERENT CULTURES OF KOREA. I LET HER STAY THERE TO STUD—

I'M GOING TO KIMHAE NOW, AND...
THAT'S ENOUGH, MOTHER.
...I'M BRINGING CHAE-KYUNG BACK AND PUTTING AN END TO THIS EXILE.
W- WHAT?!
YUL—!
YUL—!
I SEE, CHAE-JUN. WHAT CAN YOU DO? THERE'LL BE ANOTHER TIME.
GIVE MY LOVE TO THE FOLKS, OKAY?

MY BODY'S IN ROUGH SHAPE...
THE ANEMIA IS WORSE...
HALT
멈칫
GRAB
턱
AGAIN...
UHH
어

YUL—!
WHEN DID YOU GET HERE? YOU DIDN'T TELL ME YOU WERE COMING.

WHY THE SAD FACE? I CAME ALL THE WAY HERE TO SEE YOU.
WAS THAT A GOOD IDEA? I THOUGHT THAT IF THE CROWN PRINCE WASN'T IN THE PALACE, THE SECOND IN LINE HAD TO BE...
WELL, THAT'S THE RULE...
...BUT I REALLY MISSED YOU. YOU'RE A GOOD REASON TO BREAK ANY RULE.

BY THE WAY, CHAE-KYUNG...
...WHAT'S UP WITH THESE TINY WRISTS?
HOW MUCH WEIGHT HAVE YOU LOST?
I HAVEN'T LOST ANY...
WELL, I'M ON A DIET, SO MAYBE A LITTLE...
TELL ME THE TRUTH. IS IT THE STRESS OF LIVING IN THE PALACE? OR IS IT BECAUSE MY MOTHER'S SO MEAN?
OR...
...IS IT BECAUSE OF SHIN?

ARE YOU GETTING TIRED OF A MEAN HUSBAND WHO HASN'T CALLED OR E-MAILED FOR TWENTY DAYS—?!
......
SELFISH BASTARD—!
—!
IF WE'D GOTTEN MARRIED AND YOU WERE MY WIFE...
...I WOULD NEVER HAVE LET THIS HAPPEN TO YOU.

YOU'RE SAD ALL THE TIME AND YOU'RE WASTING AWAY...
...I WOULD NEVER HAVE LET THIS HAPPEN TO YOU!

THE ROYAL PALACE
Goong

NO, PLEASE DON'T CRY...

에취
ACHOO
SHE IS SUCH A MOOD KILLER...
AM I GETTING A COLD...?

HA

IF YOU HADN'T COME...

...I MIGHT HAVE RUN AWAY...
...RATHER THAN BE ALONE HERE ANOTHER MINUTE.
THANK YOU...
...FOR COMING BEFORE IT WAS TOO LATE.

THANK YOU FOR NOT LETTING ME RUN AWAY.

PRINCE YUL WENT TO KIMHAE PALACE—?
YES, YOUR HIGHNESS.
THE MAYOR AND THE GOVERNOR WILL SEE THE CROWN PRINCESS OFF. HER HIGHNESS AND PRINCE YUL WILL COME BACK TO SEOUL RIDING THE ROYAL TRAIN.
HOW DID THIS HAPPEN—? PRINCE YUL IS THE SECOND IN LINE FOR THE THRONE. HE HAS TO BE IN THE PALACE WHEN PRINCE SHIN IS NOT HERE.
WHY HAS HE GONE TO KIMHAE PALACE TO SEE THE CROWN PRINCESS? SHE'S TRAVELING ALONE—!

PRINCE YUL IS PRINCESS CHAE-KYUNG'S CLASSMATE. THEY ARE CLOSE LIKE SIBLINGS.
HE PROBABLY COULDN'T ENDURE PRINCESS CHAE-KYUNG'S LONELINESS.
SHUT
탁
COULD IT BE...?
WHAT DO YOU MEAN, "CATCHING A PRINCE WITH DRUGS IS TOO BIG TO EXPOSE"—?!

MOST OF THE ARTICLES DIDN'T EVEN MENTION PRINCE SHIN. NO ONE BELIEVES THE GOSSIP RAGS, NOT SINCE PRINCESS DIANA'S ACCIDENT.
QUEEN ELIZABETH HERSELF MADE SURE THE PRESS WOULD NOT KNOW ABOUT THIS.
AND NO ONE WANTS TO TOUCH A STORY THAT COULD CAUSE A DIPLOMATIC CRISIS BETWEEN TWO COUNTRIES.
OF COURSE, ONCE THE TABLOIDS AND GOSSIP COLUMNISTS HEARD THE POLICE WERE CALLED, THEY MADE SOME EDUCATED GUESSES.

THE SAME DRUGS THAT WERE FOUND IN HIS POSSESSION.
REGARDLESS, HIS DRINK TESTED POSITIVE FOR NARCOTICS.
I'LL HAVE TO BIDE MY TIME, THEN.

...THAT WILL PUT PRINCE SHIN IN A DIFFICULT SITUATION EVEN HE CAN'T WRIGGLE OUT OF.
BUT, YOUR HIGHNESS... I HAVE SOMETHING...
PRINCESS CHAE-KYUNG VISITED A HOSPITAL IN KIMHAE TO COMFORT ITS PATIENTS.
HERE WE SEE THE PRINCESS WELCOMED BY HOSPITAL STAFF.

SINCE MORE PEOPLE HAVE ACCESS TO KIMHAE PALACE THAN GYEONGBOK PALACE ...
...A LOT OF CITIZENS HAVE COME TO WITNESS PRINCESS CHAE-KYUNG'S DEPARTURE.

DOES SHE... LOOK LIKE SHE'S LOSING WEIGHT?
HMM...HER CHEEKS LOOK SALLOW.

WHEN SHE BECAME THE CROWN PRINCESS, SHE WAS ON TV A LOT. PEOPLE WERE CONGRATULATING HER ON HER WEDDING.
LIKE THE PRIME MINISTER AND OTHER DIPLOMATS AND CONGRESSMEN...
SHE LOOKED UNCOMFORTABLE... SHE NEVER LEFT THE CROWN PRINCE'S SIDE AND SEEMED AWKWARD. EVERY TIME I SAW HER, IT MADE ME NERVOUS.

BUT NOW...
...SHE LOOKS CONFIDENT AND COMFORTABLE WITH MEETING PEOPLE...

I ALWAYS PRAYED THAT SHE WOULD GET USED TO THE ROYAL LIFE...
...BUT WATCHING CHAE-KYUNG'S TRANSFORMATION...

...MAKES ME THINK...
...SHE'S NOT LIKE US ANYMORE...

AH—I'M FINALLY BACK AT GYEONGBOK PALACE~!

I'VE ONLY LIVED HERE FOR A FEW MONTHS, BUT...
...I REALLY MISSED THIS PLACE—
OH, RIGHT. WILLIAM—!

HOW HAVE THINGS BEEN GOING WHILE I WAS AWAY?
I HAVE BEEN WELL. I MISSED YOU A LOT, THOUGH...

I HAD SO MUCH FUN—
IT WAS FANTASTIC. I DON'T WANT TO GO BACK TO ENGLAND. HA-HA-HA!
HA-HA-HA...
DID HE FORGET THAT I DON'T UNDERSTAND ENGLISH?
OH, I HAVE...
...SOME NOT-SO-GOOD NEWS.
WH-WH-WHAT—?
SHIN DID WHAT—?

I AM SURE YOUR SECRETARY OR SOMEONE WILL INFORM YOU...
...BUT I'D RATHER TELL YOU MYSELF SO YOU CAN GET THE FULL DETAILS.
WHO WOULD DO SUCH THING?
TRANSLATING
THERE'S NO WAY SHIN WOULD DO THAT! IT'S PROBABLY AN ANTI-ROYALIST PLOT!
WELL, THERE IS ONE SUSPECT...
...BUT WE HAVE NO EVIDENCE.
PRINCE SHIN WILL COME BACK TO KOREA EARLIER THAN PLANNED, SO WE'LL GET THE STORY FROM HIM.
PLEASE DON'T WORRY... EVERYTHING WILL BE OKAY.

WE'LL TALK MORE LATER.
WHERE ARE YOU GOING, WILLIAM?
EUNUCH KONG RENTED SOME DVDs, AND...
...WE'RE GOING TO WATCH THEM TOGETHER~. ♡
MY POOR SHIN... MY SHIN...
STOP IT, WILLIAM. THIS IS NOT WHO YOU ARE!
DID YOU FALL FOR THAT OLD MAN'S EVIL TRICKS—?
BUT WHEN I NEEDED SOMEONE...
...HE WAS THE ONLY ONE WHO STAYED BY MY SIDE.

I KNOW... YOU GUYS MUST THINK...
...I'M WEIRD, BUT...
*TRADITIONAL KOREAN SONGS
THAT ONE IS MY STAR AND THE OTHER ONE IS...
HEE HEE.
SHH, DON'T SAY A WORD.
DID YOU... STAY HERE... ALL NIGHT FOR ME...?
...WHENEVER I WAS HOMESICK OR LONELY...
HA-HA-HA-HA. WAIT FOR ME, KONG~!
CATCH ME~!
...AND WHEN I FAINTED AFTER THAT EIGHT-HOUR PANSORI* MASTER PERFORMANCE, IT WAS EUNUCH KONG WHO STAYED WITH ME...

KONG!
HEE HEE HEE HEE... DARLING!
WHAT THE HELL IS WRONG WITH THEM...?

THE CROWN PRINCE WILL ARRIVE AROUND 3 P.M.
UNLIKE AT HIS DEPARTURE, THERE WILL BE NO PUBLIC WELCOMING CEREMONY. PEOPLE SPECULATE THAT HIS HIGHNESS HAS COME BACK EARLY...

...BECAUSE DAEWANG-DAEBI'S BIRTHDAY IS SOON.
BADUM

YESTERDAY, HIS HIGHNESS WAS—

THE CROWN PRINCE HAS ARRIVED, YOUR HIGHNESS—
I SAID I CAN'T GO—!
YOUR HIGHNESS...
YOU WERE NOT ABLE TO SEE THE PRINCE OFF WHEN HE LEFT... HIS MAJESTY IS YOUR HUSBAND...

WE'LL GO NOW. PLEASE REST UP.
SHUT

ISN'T SHE FEELING WELL...?
I SHOULD PREPARE SOME HERBAL MEDICINE...

I'LL SEE HIM AT DINNER. YOU MAY LEAVE.

ARE YOU GETTING TIRED OF A MEAN HUSBAND WHO HASN'T CALLED OR E-MAILED FOR TWENTY DAYS—?
WITH THE INVESTIGATION, PRINCE SHIN HAS HAD A DIFFICULT TIME IN ENGLAND.

드르륵
SLIDE
I CAN'T BELIEVE...
...HOW IMPATIENT I AM—

YOUR HIGHNESS, WE WILL ACCOMPANY YOU. YOUR CONDITION IS POOR—
PLEASE LISTEN, YOUR HIGHNESS—
I'M OKAY.
I'LL BE BACK.
WHICH WAY WILL SHIN COME FROM? WILL HE COME THROUGH IL-HWA GATE?

BUT...
...WHY AM I CRYING?
STUPID GIRL...
I SHOULD NEVER CRY IN FRONT OF SHIN, OR HE'LL THINK I'M STUPID TOO.
RUSTLE
바스락

STOP RIGHT THERE—!
WHY ARE YOU SO SKINNY...? YOU LOOK LIKE A SKELETON.
ARE YOU HERE FOR ME? LET ME SEE YOUR FACE UP CLOS—
STAY WHERE YOU ARE. IF YOU GET ANY CLOSER...
...YOU'RE DEAD MEAT—!

I'M DIS-
APPOINTED—
YOU KEEP YOUR HUSBAND AT ARM'S LENGTH AFTER BEING APART FOR SO LONG—?

I HEARD WHAT YOU WENT THROUGH IN ENGLAND... SO I WANTED TO...
...GREET YOU WITH A BIG SMILE, BUT...

HAVEN'T YOU EVER WATCHED ROMANTIC TV SHOWS?
YOU MIGHT HAVE A LOT TO SAY, BUT AT A TIME LIKE THIS...

...YOU SHOULD JUST JUMP INTO YOUR HUSBAND'S ARMS AND NOT SAY ANYTHING.
YOU'RE SO ANNOYING.

YOU'RE SELF-CENTERED AND ARROGANT.
YOU DON'T CARE HOW OTHER PEOPLE FEEL...
YOU'RE THE MOST ANNOYING GUY IN THE WORLD.
BUT STILL...

...I MISSED YOU...

WHAT AM I SUPPOSED TO DO IN A SITUATION LIKE THIS...?

IF SHE WANTED TO HOLD ME, SHE SHOULD'VE GRABBED ME TIGHTER. WHY'S SHE SO TENTATIVE?

더 어색하잖아……!
THIS JUST GETS MORE AWKWARD...!

ANYWAY, NEXT TIME...
...WE'LL DO IT RIGHT AND GO TOGETHER.

하 HA
하 HA
하 HA
하 HA
하 HA
HA-HA-HA-HA. KONG, YOU'RE TOO SLOW~
AHH, WAIT FOR ME, PRINCE WILLIAM~
OH...
YOU'RE BACK, PRINCE SHIN. I WAS GOING TO THE GREAT HALL~.
YOU ARE FINALLY HOME, YOUR HIGHNESS~. I MISSED YOU~.

YOU HAVE TO PROTECT ME FROM THEM~ MY SWEET PRINCE~. AHHHH~!
MY, MY, MY. PRINCE YUL AND PRINCE WILLIAM WERE FIGHTING OVER ME WHILE YOU WERE GONE, YOUR HIGHNESS~.
DAMN IT... IT'S THAT CURSED OLD MAN AGAIN...
HUH?
WILL WE EVER DO IT...?
JUST... LET'S GO TO MY QUARTERS~
WHY ARE YOU DOING THIS TO ME, YOUR HIGHNESS~?
LA-LA-LA-LA-LA...
IT'S TIME TO GO BACK TO ENGLAND...
SOMEONE PLEASE BOOK ME A TICKET ASAP...

HO-HO-HO.
DID YOU HAVE A GOOD TIME—?
YES, I DID. I CAME BACK EARLY BECAUSE I MISSED YOU.
HO-HO-HO-HO. NOT YOUR WIFE? BY THE WAY, WHERE IS THE CROWN PRINCESS...?
SHE HAS NOT BEEN WELL, SO SHE IS GETTING A CHECKUP AT THE ROYAL HOSPITAL.
I HEARD THAT YOU WERE IN A DIFFICULT SITUATION IN ENGLAND.

YES, INDEED I WAS.
SOMEONE PULLED A DIRTY TRICK ON ME.
IT COULD HAVE BEEN A BIG PROBLEM. YOU ARE LUCKY THAT THE MEDIA KEPT QUIET.
IF THE STORY GETS OUT, YOU WILL HAVE EMBARRASSED US ON THE WORLD STAGE.
TRUE, BUT I WOULDN'T WORRY ABOUT IT.
AS LONG AS A CERTAIN SOMEONE KEEPS HER MOUTH SHUT—

...HE'S JUST LIKE HIS FATHER WAS WHEN THE KING WAS YOUNG.
HE MAY BE HIDING HIS CLAWS...
I THOUGHT HE WAS MERELY A CHILD, BUT...
IT'S THE FIRST SNOW. FIRST SNOW~!
IT'S SNOWING! SNOW~!!

AIEEE, I LOVE IT~!
YOUR HIGHNESS, PLEASE TAKE AN UMBRELLA~!
탁
TRIP
철푸덕
THUD
OUCH, THAT HURT.
WHAT'RE YOU DOING? ON YOUR FEET.

WHAP
TH-THANKS...
NOT AT ALL—
HEH! WHY WOULD I BE NICE TO YOU?
YOU, YOU~ WHAT THE HELL ARE YOU DOING~?
WHAP
GET ME IF YOU CAN, SLOWPOKE!

FROM A DISTANCE, THEY LOOK LIKE THIS.

I HEARD THAT THE CROWN PRINCE HAD SOME TROUBLE...
OH, YOU MEAN HIS BRITISH SCANDAL, UNCLE?

IT COULD BE AN ANTI-MONARCH-IST PLOT OR JUST A SCHOOLBOY PRANK.
IT'S OBVIOUS PRINCE SHIN WASN'T RESPONSIBLE, YOUR HIGHNESS.
I AM SO FRUS-TRATED— WHY DO THESE THINGS ALWAYS HAPPEN TO PRINCE SHIN?
BUT UNCLE, HE HAS MADE SO MANY ERRORS IN JUDGMENT. HE MAY BE MY SON, BUT IN THIS CASE, THE FRUIT HAS FALLEN TOO FAR FROM THE ROYAL TREE.

YOU ALWAYS COMPLAIN ABOUT PRINCE SHIN AND IMPLY THAT YOU COULD APPOINT A DIFFERENT CROWN PRINCE AT ANY TIME.
ARE YOU...
...THINKING OF SOMEONE ELSE AS THE CROWN PRINCE, YOUR HIGHNESS—?
UNCLE—!
IF YOU'RE THINKING ABOUT APPOINTING PRINCE YUL AS THE CROWN PRINCE BECAUSE YOU FEEL GUILTY ABOUT YOUR LATE BROTHER...
...I, AS THE HEAD OF THE ROYAL RELATIVES...
...WILL PROTECT PRINCE SHIN.

WHY DID YOU GO OUT THEN-?
THE FORECAST SAYS IT'S THE COLDEST DAY OF THE YEAR. I THOUGHT I'D FREEZE TO DEATH.
TO FEED KYUNG-BOK.
BY THE WAY, WHY DO YOU ONLY USE YOUR SUMMER BEDROOM? WHY DON'T YOU MOVE TO THE SOUTHERN ROOM WITH THE HEATED FLOOR?

I'M GOING TO MY ROOM.
BUT THIS ROOM IS TOO COLD. I NEED WARMTH.

IF I SLEEP ON THE FLOOR, IT HURTS MY BACK...
THE MOST IMPORTANT THING FOR A MAN IS HIS BACK...
I LIKE TO SLEEP IN A BED.

THEN...

...WHY DON'T YOU COME INSIDE FOR A WHILE?
DON'T PRETEND TO BE SHOCKED... WE SHARED THE SAME BED FOR TWO WEEKS THAT TIME BEFORE, FAUX-NAÏF.
!
WHAT?

BUT...
THE TOP LAYER OF THIS BED IS A HEATED STONE MATTRESS. IT'S QUITE WARM.
...MAY I...?
TH-THEN...
EXCUSE ME...
SOMEONE TOLD ME SOMETHING.
WAS I...
...ORIGINALLY SUPPOSED TO MARRY YUL?

......
MY GRANDFATHER PROMISED YOUR GRANDFATHER THAT YOU WOULD MARRY WHICHEVER PRINCE BECAME KING.
BACK THEN, YUL WAS THE ROYAL GRANDSON.
RIGHT.
YOU WERE YUL'S FIANCÉE.

I SEE...
SINCE I FOUND OUT, IT'S BEEN AWKWARD AROUND YUL.

YUL MUST HAVE BEEN SO NICE TO YOU. HE HAS THE BEST MANNERS TOWARD GIRLS.
I UNDERSTAND HOW DISAPPOINTED YOU MUST BE...
...THAT YUL ISN'T YOUR HUSBAND...

SHE HAS LOST NINE POUNDS.
SHE DOES NOT EAT HER MEALS...
WE KEEP ASKING HER TO TAKE HERBAL MEDICINE, BUT SHE KEEPS DODGING US...
WHAT SHOULD WE DO, YOUR HIGHNESS—?

WHAT ...
...MAKES YOU SO UNHAPPY?
YOUR HIGHNESS, YOU SHOULD NOT GO IN—
!
LET GO OF ME—!
MM...
IT IS IMPROPER FOR YOU TO HINDER ME!!
SLIDE
!

PRINCE, WE NEED TO TAL—

W-WHAT ON EARTH ARE YOU TWO DOING...?
WHAT DO YOU MEAN, MOTHER?
I-IT'S NOT LIKE—
THIS IS THE CROWN PRINCE'S QUARTERS. IT'S MY PRIVATE ROOM. HOW COULD YOU BARGE INTO MY CHAMBERS LIKE THIS?

EVEN IF YOU ARE MY MOTHER, THERE IS ETIQUETTE TO BE FOLLOWED, ISN'T THERE?
BESIDES, WE...
...HAVEN'T DONE THE THINGS YOU'RE IMAGINING, SO STOP LOOKING AT US LIKE THAT.
CHAE-KYUNG WAS FREEZING COLD, SO SHE CLIMBED INTO BED TO GET WARM.
DO YOU THINK YOU ARE IN ANY POSITION TO SPEAK TO ME THAT WAY?
LOOK AT THIS. THIS IS AN ENGLISH GOSSIP MAGAZINE!

DID YOU REALLY PAY FOR HER AIRPLANE TICKET AND HOTEL?
IS THIS ARTICLE TRUE?
WHY WOULD YOU DO THAT? WHY—?
EVERYONE IS WATCHING YOU, WAITING TO SEE HOW YOU CONDUCT YOURSELF IN THE WORLD.
HOW COULD YOU BE SO THOUGHTLESS, CROWN PRINCE?

WE SHOULD NOT DISCUSS THIS IN FRONT OF HER. COME TO MY QUARTERS AND EXPLAIN YOURSELF.
TURN

WHAT IS IT? WHAT'S GOING ON—?
WHAT DOES THE ARTICLE SAY—

WHY IS SHE SO MAD...?

PRINCE'

MD

...YOU SAW HER...? SHE WAS IN ENGLAND?
SHE CAME THROUGH ENGLAND AS PART OF HER WINTER VACATION.
SHE SAID SHE CAME TO WATCH A BALLET COMPETITION.

...WHY DID YOU PAY FOR HER HOTEL AND PLANE TICKET...?
THEN...
WHY DID YOU DO THAT FOR HER? WHAT DOES SHE MEAN TO YOU?
DO I HAVE TO REPORT EVERY LITTLE THING I DO TO YOU NOW?
I...I WAS INVOLVED IN SOMETHING VERY STUPID IN ENGLAND.
I NEEDED A FRIEND I COULD TALK TO, EVEN IF JUST FOR AN HOUR. HYO-RIN CAME TO SEE ME AT THE RIGHT TIME, AND I WAS THANKFUL.

MY FRIEND NEEDED ME TOO. SHE WAS BROKE.
WASN'T THAT THE RIGHT THING TO DO? TO HELP SOMEONE WHEN THEY NEEDED IT? OR SHOULD I FIND ANOTHER EXCUSE FOR YOU?
WHY'RE YOU SO UPSET ABOUT IT?
THERE'S A PICTURE OF YOU AND ANOTHER WOMAN.
I CAN'T WONDER WHY? IF THE SHOE WAS ON THE OTHER FOOT, WOULDN'T YOU?

I...
...DON'T WANT YOU TO WORRY.

WHAT DO YOU CARE ABOUT SOMEONE AS INSIGNIFICANT AS ME?
IT'S YOU WHO SHOULDN'T WORRY. I'M HEALTHY.

YOU JUST FOCUS ON YOUR HEALTH AND DON'T WORRY ABOUT ME.

YOU'RE HEALTHY—?
GRAB
YOUR ARMS ARE AS THIN AS A MOSQUITO'S LEGS, AND YOU'RE TELLING ME YOU'RE HEALTHY—?
WHAT'S GOT YOU SO WORRIED THAT YOU CAN'T EVEN EAT?!
DO YOU KNOW HOW MANY PEOPLE AROUND HERE ARE WORRIED ABOUT YOU? WHAT'S YOUR PROBLEM?

SNAP
MY WORRIES ARE NO CONCERN OF YOURS.
WHAT?
IF I CAN'T ASK YOU ABOUT A TABLOID PHOTOGRAPH, THEN WHY SHOULD YOU GET TO CARE IF I STARVE TO DEATH OR NOT? HUH?
CHAE-KYUNG SHIN...
I'M SUCH AN IDIOT...

YOU LOOK HAPPY IN THE PICTURE. HAPPY WITH HER...
...WHEN I COULDN'T SLEEP BECAUSE I WAS CONCERNED ABOUT YOU AND WHAT HAPPENED. BUT I CAN SEE I WAS STUPID AND PATHETIC TO GIVE YOU SO MUCH THOUGHT!
SLAM
SIGH

MEANWHILE, THE BRITISH ARTICLE FOUND ITS WAY TO THE KOREAN PRESS CORPS.
IT AFFECTED THE YOUTH MORE THAN IT DID THE ELDER GENERATION. ALL THE KIDS WERE TALKING ABOUT IT.
ONCE SCHOOL STARTED, THE GOSSIP WAS EVERYWHERE.
THE ROYAL FAMILY WAS HAVING A HARD TIME SQUASHING THE RUMOR THAT THE CROWN PRINCE AND THE CROWN PRINCESS WERE HAVING MARITAL PROBLEMS.
WITH EACH RETELLING, THE STORY GREW BIGGER, MORE EXAGGERATED.

HEY, CHAE-KYUNG~!
ARE YOU OKAY~?

SURE. WHY~?
HOW CAN YOU ASK WHY WHEN EVERYONE'S BUZZING ABOUT THE CROWN PRINCE CHEATING ON YOU IN ENGLAND WITH HYO-RIN?

CHEATING ON ME~? DON'T BE SILLY.
HYO-RIN WENT TO SEE A BALLET COMPETITION IN ENGLAND.
SINCE SHE WAS THERE, SHE WENT TO SEE SHIN. THEY'VE BEEN FRIENDS SINCE JUNIOR HIGH.

STILL, THAT DIRTY MINX MUST HAVE FLIRTED WITH HIM~. SHE SHOULDN'T HAVE VISITED WITH THE CROWN PRINCE ALONE.
HEH
NO WAY~.
KIDS ARE STARTING TO SAY YOU'RE THE NEW PRINCESS DIANA AND HAVE BULIMIA BECAUSE THE CROWN PRINCE IS SKANKING AROUND. THEY SAY THAT'S WHY YOU GOT SO SKINNY.
I'M JUST OVERWORKED AND HAVE NO APPETITE. I'M ALWAYS OUT LATE. JUST LAST NIGHT WAS THE EMBASSY PARTY.
YOU KNOW ME. I'M A LAZY BUM. THIS BUSY LIFE IS SUPER HARD FOR ME~.

I DON'T UNDERSTAND YOUR HUSBAND, THOUGH. WHY DID HE LEND THAT GIRL MONEY? THAT'S WHY EVERYONE'S TALKING ABOUT IT~.
YOU'D BETTER KEEP YOUR EYE ON HIM OR THAT WENCH WILL WEASEL HER WAY IN. OKAY?

SO YOU AND YOUR HUSBAND ARE GETTING ALONG ALL RIGHT?
......

HAVE WE EVER GOTTEN ALONG...?

REGARDLESS, PLEASE EAT BETTER~
DON'T BE LIKE A WIFE WHO'S PUNISHING HERSELF FOR THE SINS OF HER HUSBAND~
...HA-HA. OKAY, OKAY~
THE INCIDENT...
...HAS GROWN SO BIG.
SHIN AND I ARE PUBLIC FIGURES, SO WE HAVE NO CONTROL OVER THESE THINGS, BUT HYO-RIN IS DIFFERENT...

KIDS GOSSIP BEHIND HER BACK, AND HER PARENTS MUST KNOW ABOUT THIS BY NOW...
IT'S HER—!!
IT'S HYO-RIN—
OH...
HI.
UH, HI.

WHAT SHOULD DO?
SHE'S... WALKING AWAY.
HEY—

CAN WE TALK?

HEY~!
BIG NEWS, BIG NEWS~!

WHAT?
WHAT'S THE RUCKUS~?
WELL, IT'S...
CH-CHAE-KYUNG...

OUR CROWN PRINCESS HAS FINALLY CHALLENGED HYO-RIN TO A DUEL~!!

WHAT DID YOU SAY~?
HOW?
WHAT DO YOU MEAN~?
HUH?
SOMEONE SAW CHAE-KYUNG AND HYO-RIN TALKING IN THE BACK FIELD~!
WHAT~?
A WICKED STORM IS BREWING.
WHAT SHOULD WE DO, SHIN?
SHOULDN'T YOU GO AND STOP THEM?
RIGHT. IF THEY FIGHT OVER YOU...
I ENVY YOU... TWO GIRLS DOING BATTLE TO WIN YOUR HEART...

...I'M NOT INTERESTED IN THIS ONE.
IT'S FUN TO WATCH A FIGHT BETWEEN TWO GIRLS, BUT...
IT'S TOO OBVIOUS WHAT CHAE-KYUNG WILL DO.
SOMETHING ABOUT HIM IS DARK... VERY DARK...
WHAT THE...? HE'S ACTING LIKE IT DOESN'T CONCERN HIM.
LA-LA-LA.
SHIN TOLD ME WHAT REALLY HAPPENED IN ENGLAND.
UH...THINGS MUST BE PRETTY TOUGH FOR YOU THESE DAYS, HUH? ARE YOUR PARENTS MAD?
THE TABLOIDS EXAGGERATE EVERYTHING.

WAIT!!
HOLD ON.
WE'LL HELP YOU, CHAE-KYUNG.
YOU'RE TOO WEAK TO FIGHT ALONE.
CHEW
질겅
질겅
CHEW
W-WHAT'RE YOU GUYS DOING?
IN YOUR WEAKENED STATE, YOU'RE NO MATCH FOR HER SPORTY PHYSIQUE. LEAVE THIS TO US.
JUST GO OVER THERE AND WATCH.
SO~ YOU'RE HYO-RIN?
WHAT'RE YOU DOING?! GO AWAY!
WE HEARD YOU WENT TO ENGLAND TO FLIRT WITH THE CROWN PRINCE.
SMILE
피식
SMILE?
S-SMILE?
HA-HA-HA...
SHE JUST SMILED...
FORGET THE GUM...
PTUI
퉤
...I'LL CHEW YOU UP INSTEAD.

COME ON, BABY~.
CRACK
HUH?
DAMN IT. THE GUM'S STUCK IN MY HAIR. LOOK AT THIS!
STRETCH
S-SERIOUSLY...?
WAHHHH~
WHAT SHOULD I DO? WHAT SHOULD I DO~?
I WENT TO A HAIR SALON YESTERDAY AND GOT THIS NEW STYLE~
DON'T COME CLOSE TO ME. I DON'T WANT GUM IN MY HAIR.
PUT PEANUT BUTTER ON IT~
HEY—
WHO ARE THEY...?
W-WHY DID THEY EVEN COME...? THEY JUST MADE THINGS WORSE...

HA-HA, SORRY. THOSE WERE MY FRIENDS...
THEY'RE ALL MIXED UP.

THEY'RE SUCH DRAMA QUEENS. I'M REALLY SORRY.
THEY'RE STILL THERE...
WAHHH~

ANYWAY, I...SO...SO...
I CAN'T THINK...
I WAS WORRIED THAT YOU WERE IN TROUBLE...

...BUT THESE KINDS OF STORIES GO AWAY QUICKLY, SO DON'T WORRY.
DON'T LISTEN TO WHAT OTHER KIDS SAY.
I KNOW YOU ONLY WENT TO SEE SHIN BECAUSE YOU WERE ALREADY IN ENGLAND...
I'M SORRY, BUT...
...THAT'S NOT TRUE. WHO TOLD YOU THAT?
WHAT?
THE ONLY REASON I WENT TO ENGLAND WAS TO SEE SHIN.
I HAD A LOT TO TALK TO HIM ABOUT, BUT I NEVER HAD A CHANCE BECAUSE YOU WERE ALWAYS AROUND.

WE USED TO HAVE DEEP CONVERSATIONS ALL THE TIME. I'VE MISSED THAT SINCE HE GOT MARRIED.
SHIN WAS IN A BAD SPOT OVER THERE, AND HE SEEMED HAPPY TO SEE ME.
BY THE WAY, SINCE WE'RE OPENING UP HERE...
...I FEEL LIKE YOU'RE ACCUSING ME OF BEING SHIN'S MISTRESS.
W-WHAT DO YOU MEAN? HOW COULD YOU SAY THAT—?
THINK ABOUT IT. YOU'RE GIVING ME ADVICE AND PRETENDING TO BE WORRIED ABOUT ME...
I FEEL STRANGE...
...BUT YOU REALLY JUST WANT TO FIND OUT WHAT ACTUALLY HAPPENED, DON'T YOU?

HOW COULD YOU THINK THAT...? THAT'S NOT TRUE...
WHY...
...IS EVERYTHING GETTING BLURRY?
YOU... DON'T LOOK SO GOOD.
ARE YOU SICK?
S-SORRY, BUT WE'LL HAVE TO TALK LATER.
I'M NOT FEELING UP TO IT RIGHT NOW...
휘청
WOBBLE
UH...

TAP
TAP
TAP
TAP
SLAM
HUFF
HUFF
C-COME QUICK...

...CHAE-KYUNG
HAS FAINTED—!

NO WAY. CH-CHAE-KYUNG FAINTED?!
WHAT HAPPENED? IT'S SO SUDDEN—
SHOULD WE CALL 911?
TAKE HER TO THE SCHOOL NURSE...
NO, THERE'S NO TIME FOR THAT.
WE'LL WATCH OVER HER. AN AMBULANCE WILL BE HERE SOON.
WHAT'S GOING ON? WHAT HAPPENED TO HER?
WE'LL TAKE HER TO OUR CAR. CAN YOU PLEASE...
...BRING SOME WARM WATER AND A COLD, WET TOWEL?

WE DON'T HAVE TIME TO WAIT FOR AN AMBULANCE. SHE'S CONSCIOUS AT LEAST. LET'S DRIVE HER TO THE HOSPITAL OURSELVES.
YES, YOUR HIGHNESS.
YOUR HIGHNESS... WE JUST GOT HERE. WE DON'T KNOW THE STORY YET.
I'M FINE. I FEEL BETTER...
WHAT HAPPENED WAS—

HE...
WHAT THE HELL...? IS SHE CRYING?
HE...
WHAT THE...? I THOUGHT THEY WEREN'T GETTING ALONG, BUT THE CROWN PRINCE ACTS LIKE HE REALLY CARES...
BY THE WAY, WHAT DID HYO-RIN DO THAT MADE CHAE-KYUNG FAINT?
THAT'S WHAT I WANNA KNOW... HYO-RIN ACTS LIKE A LADY, BUT IT'S ALL JUST AN ACT~.

...DIDN'T LOOK AT ME EVEN ONCE—
MM...

...I CAN
RELY ON...
THE ONLY
PERSON...

YOU AWAKE?
HOW'RE YOU FEELING?
SO-SO.
AREN'T YOU HUNGRY? DO YOU WANNA EAT SOMETHING?
...NO THANKS ...
WHAT CAN I DO...

...TO MAKE YOU EAT?
탁
WHAM
PLEASE KNOCK FIRST...
MOM—!

HOW...HOW...?
DO YOU KNOW HOW WORRIED I'VE BEEN? WHY AREN'T YOU EATING? WHY—?
MOM—
I AM ALWAYS SICK WITH WORRY, AND NOW YOU—
MOM, STOP IT~. WHERE ARE DAD AND CHAE-JUN?
WITH GRANDPA AT YOUR GREAT-AUNT'S 60TH BIRTHDAY PARTY...
SHUT

HOW DO YOU FEEL?
YOU'RE LIKE THE NEW "IT GIRL" ALL OF A SUDDEN—
I GUESS OTHER PEOPLE THINK "THE CROWN PRINCE'S EX-GIRLFRIEND" IS A COOL THING TO BE.
EVEN THOUGH GIRLS TALK BEHIND YOUR BACK, BOYS ARE CRAZY ABOUT YOU. YOU MUST BE THRILLED.
I GUESS. MORE LIKE SURPRISED, REALLY.
OUR PHONE AT HOME IS RINGING OFF THE HOOK WITH REPORTERS CALLING FOR INTERVIEWS AND TALENT AGENTS TRYING TO SCOUT ME.

SHOULDN'T YOU BE THANKING ME?
IF THESE THINGS KEEP HAPPENING TO SHIN, IT'LL BE EASIER FOR YOU TO TAKE THE THRONE FROM HIM.
WHY DO I GET THE FEELING YOU'RE ANGRY WITH ME INSTEAD?
IS IT THE ACHING IN YOUR HEART THAT MAKES YOU BLIND TO YOUR ALLIES?
I KNOW YOU SECRETLY LOVE CHAE-KYUNG. ARE YOU MAD BECAUSE YOU THINK I HURT HER?

SO... I WOULD LIKE TO TAKE CHAE-KYUNG HOME FOR A WHILE, YOUR HIGHNESS.
I THINK SHE WILL RECOVER FASTER IF SHE HAS HER FAMILY BY HER SIDE.
......
I'M SORRY, BUT I CAN'T LET YOU DO THAT.

IT'S NOT THAT I DON'T THINK SHE'LL BE BETTER OFF GOING WITH YOU, BUT IF SHE GETS WORSE AFTER SHE COMES BACK...
...ARE YOU GOING TO TAKE HER AWAY YET AGAIN?
UH, I DON'T—
BECAUSE OF RECENT EVENTS, IT'S LITTLE BIT CHAOTIC ON OUR SIDE OF THE PALACE.
THE CROWN PRINCESS IS NEEDED HERE.
BUT THE QUEEN ALREADY ALLOWED HER—
CHAE-KYUNG IS MY WIFE.

IT'S THE CROWN PRINCE WHO MAKES DECISIONS FOR THE CROWN PRINCESS.
OUR DOCTORS AND FACILITIES ARE THE BEST IN THE COUNTRY...
...SO PLEASE DON'T WORRY ABOUT HER.
YOU MAY THINK I'M BEING CRUEL, BUT I DON'T WANT TO HAVE ANY FUTURE MISUNDERSTANDINGS.
I AM CHAE-KYUNG'S GUARDIAN, NOT YOU.
EVEN IF MY MOTHER SAYS SHE CAN GO, IT'S NOT GOING TO HAPPEN IF I SAY NO.

YOUR MOTHER WENT TO THE PALACE BECAUSE MY GRANDMOTHER ASKED TO SEE HER.

YOU...
WHAP
YOU BASTARD—!!
WHO DO YOU THINK YOU ARE? HOW COULD YOU TALK TO MY MOM LIKE THAT?
IT'S BETTER FOR HER TO UNDERSTAND IT'S IMPOSSIBLE RATHER THAN GIVE HER FALSE HOPE.
IF YOU GO TO YOUR PARENTS' HOUSE EVERY TIME YOU'RE IN TROUBLE, IT WILL BECOME A CRUTCH. YOU'LL COMPLAIN MORE AT OUR HOME AND BE A PAIN IN MY ASS.
MY MOM ASKED YOU THAT BECAUSE SHE WAS WORRIED ABOUT ME. HOW COULD YOU BE SO MEAN ABOUT TURNING HER DOWN?

WE'LL ONLY GET BUSIER WHEN WE BECOME ELEVENTH GRADERS...SO I CAN'T LET YOU DO EVERY LITTLE THING YOU WANT.
ALLOW~? WHY DO I HAVE TO ASK YOUR PERMISSION?
ARE YOU SERIOUSLY CONFUSED BY THIS?
WAKE UP.
THE PALACE IS NOT THE SAME AS THE OUTSIDE WORLD.

PEOPLE OUTSIDE PURSUE EQUALITY BETWEEN THE SEXES.
PALACE LIFE, HOWEVER, IS BASED ON CONFUCIANISM.

SO WITHIN ITS WALLS, A WIFE HAS TO FOLLOW WHAT HER HUSBAND SAYS.

DON'T SKIP ANY MEALS.
CLACK
SEE YOU LATER.
BASTARD...
......
ONLY ONE THING...
I WAS ONLY THINKING ABOUT ONE THING.

IF YOU LEAVE THE PALACE AND ENJOY THE HAPPINESS OF BEING WITH YOUR FAMILY...
...I KNOW FOR CERTAIN...
...YOU WILL NEVER COME BACK TO THE PALACE—

THE REASON WE ASKED YOU TO COME HERE...
LADY HAN: HEAD CHEF OF THE ROYAL KITCHEN. (AGE UNKNOWN. - -;;)
...IS BECAUSE THE CROWN PRINCESS HAS NOT BEEN EATING WELL...
I KEEP HEARING MUSIC...
ARE YOU COMING? ARE YOU COMING? ARE YOU COMING FOREVER?
I HEAR IT TOO.
ARE YOU GOING? ARE YOU GOING? ARE YOU GOING FOREVER?*
IT IS MY RINGTONE...
*IT'S THE THEME SONG FROM A POPULAR HISTORICAL DRAMA. THE DRAMA IS ABOUT CHEFS IN THE ROYAL KITCHEN DURING THE CHOSUN DYNASTY.
ANYWAY, SINCE YOU ARE THE HEAD CHEF...
...YOU ARE ALSO RESPONSIBLE FOR THE CROWN PRINCESS'S LACK OF NOURISHMENT.
WE ASKED THE CROWN PRINCESS'S MOTHER TO COME.
SHE IS GOING TO TEACH YOU TO MAKE SOME OF HER DAUGHTER'S FAVORITE DISHES.

HMM...
SHE'S THINKING ABOUT SOMETHING...
Z Z Z.....
DON'T FALL ASLEEP!
YOUR HIGHNESS.
THE QUALITY OF FOOD IS NOT THE REASON FOR THE CROWN PRINCESS'S LACK OF APPETITE.
OF COURSE WE KNOW IT HAS NOTHING TO DO WITH THE TASTE OF YOUR COOKING.
IT'S JUST THAT SHE MAY ENJOY FOODS THAT REMIND HER OF THE COMFORTS OF HOME—
*PRINCESS YUN-JUNG: THE LATE KING'S YOUNGER SISTER. SHE IS THE QUEEN MOTHER'S SISTER-IN-LAW.
I HAVE SERVED MANY CROWN PRINCESSES FOR OVER SIXTY YEARS.
I SUPPOSE YOUR HIGHNESSES HAVE FORGOTTEN WHEN EACH ONE OF YOU WAS A CROWN PRINCESS IN MY CARE.

TERMINOLOGY OF GOONG

BIN:
AMONG THE KING'S CONCUBINES, THE CONCUBINE WHO WAS JUNG-POOM 1 RECEIVED THE TITLE OF "BIN." BUT THE CROWN PRINCESS WAS ALSO GIVEN THE TITLE OF "BIN." WHO DO YOU THINK RANKED HIGHER? THE CROWN PRINCESS, OF COURSE. A CROWN PRINCESS IS ABOVE ALL OTHER RANKS. SO THE KING'S CONCUBINES MUST HONOR THE CROWN PRINCESS, WHO IS ALSO THEIR DAUGHTER-IN-LAW.*

*ORDER OF GOVERNMENT OFFICERS

LONELINESS? BUT SHE'S SURROUNDED BY PEOPLE...
YES, BUT EVEN A HUNDRED PEOPLE WOULD BE USELESS.
THERE IS NOTHING WE CAN DO TO HELP THAT.
THE CROWN PRINCESS WILL ONLY GET BETTER WHEN HER RELATIONSHIP WITH THE CROWN PRINCE GETS BETTER.
LIVING IN THE PALACE OVER SIXTY YEARS HAS TAUGHT ME A FEW THINGS. THE TRICK IS...
...YOU HAVE TO TREAT A SICKNESS OF THE MIND WITH THE BODY AND TREAT A PHYSICAL AILMENT WITH THE MIND.
THE CROWN PRINCE AND THE CROWN PRINCESS...

...SHOULD SPEND A NIGHT TOGETHER AS SOON AS POSSIBLE—
TO BE CONTINUED IN GOONG VOL. 6!

Preview

vol. 6

Park SoHee

S-SPEND A NIGHT TOGETHER...? THEY ARE ONLY EIGHTEEN YEARS OLD,* HOW COULD THEY POSSIBLY "NEED" TO SPEND A NIGHT TOGETHER?
WE ARE DISCUSSING THE CROWN PRINCESS'S ILLNESS, NOT HER LOVE LIFE. HELP US UNDERSTAND WHAT YOU MEAN.
* THE WESTERN EQUIVALENT WOULD BE MORE LIKE SIXTEEN OR SEVENTEEN YEARS OLD.
HMM...
Z Z Z Z
STOP FALLING ASLEEP!!
**A KOREAN CARD GAME.
WAKE UP...
I OBSERVED EACH OF YOUR HIGHNESSES WHILD YOU WERE NEWLYWEDS TOO.
YOU DID NOT WANT TO EAT, AND YOU ALL LOST WEIGHT. YOUR PERIODS WERE IRREGULAR. I EVEN CAUGHT YOU TRYING TO RUN AWAY FROM THE PALACE. AH, AND WE PLAYED GO-STOP** ON A NUMBER OF OCCASIONS.
GO-STOP IS TOTALLY IRRELEVANT!!!
AND YOUR HIGHNESSES WERE ALL JUST LIKE THE CROWN PRINCESS.

REGARDLESS, YOUR HIGHNESSES COULD NOT GET USED TO PALACE LIFE, EITHER.
BUT THEN, EACH OF YOU SPENT A NIGHT WITH YOUR HUSBANDS, AND DESPITE BEING UNDERAGE...

U-UNDERAGE...? DID I REALLY...?

WELL...MY LATE HUSBAND AND I SPENT OUR FIRST NIGHT TOGETHER WHEN I WAS EIGHTEEN.
I...WAS EIGHTEEN YEARS OLD TOO. THE AWKWARDNESS BETWEEN US DISAPPEARED IMMEDIATELY AFTERWARD.
I WAS SIXTEEN YEARS OLD...THE ELDERS WANTED US TO HAVE A BABY BECAUSE THE KINGDOM WAS IN CHAOS AT THE TIME.

RIGHT, RIGHT. THAT WAS THE NIGHT...
WELL, IF IT WASN'T THE FIRST NIGHT...
HOW ELSE DID IT HAPPEN?
BLUSH
YOUR HIGHNESS!

WELL...THE FORMAL RULE IS THAT A CROWN PRINCE AND A CROWN PRINCESS SHOULD NOT BE INTIMATE UNTIL THEY ARE ADULTS...
...BUT IT'S NOT UNUSUAL FOR A YOUNG COUPLE TO SHARE A NIGHT AT AN EARLIER DATE.
HOWEVER, LADY HAN... WHAT IS...
...THE CONNECTION BETWEEN INTIMACY AND THE CROWN PRINCESS'S HEALTH?
THAT'S EASY TO EXPLAIN, YOUR HIGHNESS.

EXCEPT...
...IT'S QUITE POSSIBLE THAT EVEN IF THE CROWN PRINCE AND THE CROWN PRINCESS SPEND A NIGHT TOGETHER...
...NOTHING AT ALL WILL CHANGE. THEIR RELATIONSHIP IS...AWKWARD.
WHEN THEY VISITED HER PARENTS' HOUSE, THEY STAYED IN THE SAME ROOM AND NOTHING AT ALL HAPPENED BETWEEN THEM.

IF THAT'S THE CASE, WHY SHOULD WE PUSH THEM TO SLEEP TOGETHER?
BECAUSE...
...OF THE ATMOSPHERE IT'LL CREATE.
DON'T YOU REMEMBER THE MYSTERIOUS FEELING THAT ONLY OCCURS THE FIRST TIME? THEY WILL EXPERIENCE A STRANGE SENSE OF FREEDOM THAT ONLY THEY WILL KNOW, THAT IS BEYOND OTHER CHILDREN THEIR AGE.
THEIR NIGHT ALONE WILL INSPIRE FEELINGS OF CHANGE, A BOND EXCLUSIVE TO THEM. THE STRANGENESS OF THAT NIGHT WILL CREATE A SPECIAL AGONY, A STATE BETWEEN DESIRE AND TEMPERANCE.

AFTER THEY SPEND A NIGHT TOGETHER...
...THEY WILL OPEN THEIR HEARTS TO ONE ANOTHER.
R-RIGHT. THAT'S HOW IT WAS FOR US!!

PALACE INFORMATION

GONGJOO AND ONGJOO

A GONGJOO IS A PRINCESS WHOSE PARENTS ARE A KING AND A QUEEN, AND AN ONGJOO IS A PRINCESS WHOSE PARENTS ARE A KING AND HIS CONCUBINE. WHEN A GONGJOO OR AN ONGJOO MARRIED, IT WAS CALLED HAGA (ROUGHLY, MARRYING A PERSON LOWER IN STATUS). AND A KING'S SON-IN-LAW WAS CALLED BUMADOWI OR GOOKSEO. EVEN THOUGH THEY WERE TECHNICALLY BOTH SONS-IN-LAW TO THE KING, A GONGJOO'S HUSBAND WAS RANKED AS JUNG POOM 1 (THE HIGHEST LEVEL OF GOVERNMENT OFFICE) AND AN ONGJOO'S HUSBAND WAS RANKED JONG POOM 1 (THE SECOND HIGHEST). HUSBANDS OF EITHER A GONGJOO OR AN ONGJOO WERE NOT PERMITTED TO HAVE CONCUBINES. NEITHER A GONGJOO NOR AN ONGJOO WERE REQUIRED TO BOW TO THEIR IN-LAWS, AND THOSE IN-LAWS WERE REQUIRED TO ADDRESS THEIR DAUGHTERS-IN-LAW USING HONORIFIC TITLES.

HOW COULD YOU SAY SUCH A THING?!
BANG

WHAT?! YOU ARE A ROYAL RELATIVE, AND THUS SHOULD BE EQUALLY LOYAL TO THE KING AND THE CROWN PRINCE! WHERE DO YOU GET SUCH NERVE?
UNCLE!
CAN'T YOU SEE WHAT PRINCE SHIN IS DOING? HE IS RUINING THE ROYAL FAMILY'S REPUTATION.

TO BE HONEST...
...PRINCE YUL IS BETTER KING MATERIAL THAN THE CROWN PRINCE.

IF DAEBI-MAMA IS MANEUVERING TO MAKE PRINCE YUL THE NEXT KING, I WILL HELP HER.
THE CROWN PRINCE HAS DISAPPOINTED MANY OF THE ROYAL RELATIVES, AND THEY HAVE THROWN THEIR SUPPORT TO PRINCE YUL TOO.

PRINCE YUL HAS A LEGITIMATE CLAIM TO THE THRONE. HE IS JUST AS MUCH AN HEIR OF THE LATE KING AS PRINCE SHIN.
SHE GREW UP A COMMONER, AND THUS ISN'T GOOD ENOUGH TO BE THE NEXT QUEEN. I CAN'T BELIEVE THAT SHE BECAME THE CROWN PRINCESS BECAUSE OF A PROMISE MADE IN ERROR.
THE CROWN PRINCE WAS ON TRACK BEFORE THE MARRIAGE...
I DON'T CARE FOR THE CROWN PRINCESS, EITHER.
...BUT NOW THAT'S SHE'S HIS WIFE, HIS BEHAVIOR IS UNACCEPTABLE!

Goong vol. 5

Story and art by SoHee Park

Translation HyeYoung Im
English Adaptation Jamie S. Rich
Lettering Alexis Eckerman

Yen Press
Hachette Book Group USA
237 Park Avenue, New York, NY 10017

Visit our Web sites at www.HachetteBookGroup.com and www.YenPress.com.

Yen Press is an imprint of Hachette Book Group, Inc.
The Yen Press name and logo are trademarks of Hachette Book Group, Inc.

First Yen Press Edition: June 2009

ISBN: 978-0-7595-3123-9

10 9 8 7 6 5 4 3 2 1

BVG

Printed in the United States of America